Charm, Elegance, and Intrigue

Mark Schardine

Blue Jade Press, LLC

Blue Jade Press, LLC
Vineland, NJ 08360
www.bluejadepress.com

To the Muse who encourages us all...

Introduction

Poetry involves the use of forms, the search for a means to change an idea not merely into a coherent work, but to condense the words in a refined manner into a poem pleasing to the reader, also to present the poets' ideas with complete clarity.

The Internet site fanstory.com offers insight into many diverse poetic forms, among them the Japanese form of tanka, which allows the poet to use five lines, the first with five syllables, the second with seven syllables, the third with five, and the fourth and fifth with seven each. In this collection, each poem has a title, plus the five lines (in one instance two sets of five lines), and is a separate work.

The poet who accepts the challenge of the tanka form has only five lines and thirty-one syllables to tell a story. Each line must give its own particular insight, and by the end, the poet must present vivid images to the reader.

Although the tanka form would not seem to offer enough opportunity to go into detail about the story, the use of a few words can cause the reader's imagination to see the details, even conjure images from which the reader will not turn away.

A tanka poem can bring into sharp focus a moment that gives joy, or one that leads to sorrow, or simply one that becomes an unmistakable memory. The reader may need less than a minute to read a tanka poem, but take much time to ponder its ideas. A poem may even come to mind days, months, or years later, and cause the reader to contemplate it anew.

Table of Contents

A Bit of Ambivalence

As she looks away
Know that you are in her thoughts
She is fond of you
Finds you handsome and witty
But she does like other men.

A Brief Chat

By soft candlelight
You felt velour on your hand
Her soothing whisper
Reminded you once again
How you need her discretion.

A Chapter Ends

He sees her depart
Slowly disappear from view
Their love story ends,
She was thoughtful and discreet
All will remain unnoticed.

A Courtesan Adds to Her Income

As the sun rises
She lets him see her again
Her delicate hands
Her sly lascivious grin
As she takes from his wallet.

A Courtesan on Vacation

Cheap lodgings for now
Simple dinner with no drinks
Calm restful slumber
Still allow for seaside strolls
Her figure can change her luck.

A Life Well-Lived

He watched from afar
How she used charm and glamour
Advanced her status
Never one to be alone
This lady he once divorced.

A Point of No Return

Finding him charming
Perhaps hypnotized by him
She offers her hand
Lets his eyes stare into hers
Thinks she understands his thoughts.

A Scandal Just Broke

No words are spoken
We only hear sounds of
Soft background music
And occasional laughter
Yet everything is known.

A Wife's Revenge

She makes not a sound
Swiftly stealthily enters
His fine hotel room
Sees the couple fast asleep
Steals his mistress's diamonds.

After Strolling Downtown

Red roses clearly seen
Both her hands on his shoulders
She whispers slowly
Shows him a ring to give her
Places her hands on his heart.

All Must Be Seen

Her eyes probe your mind
Uncover each of your thoughts
Sift and assess them
Weigh and measure their contents
And never give her verdict.

Almost a Brilliant Success

She sought to please him
Offered witty compliments
Flattered lured enticed
Beckoned his eyes to meet hers
Not knowing his intentions.

Almost an Admonishment

Her hand placed on his
Calmly yet with insistence
Velvet kept in place
She coaxes and reminds him
How he enjoys her favor.

Alone with a Martini

He tempted and teased
Flattered and slowly lulled her
Saw how she gave way
Succumbed to his smooth embrace
To give him one night's pleasure.

Now she slowly sips
Recalls his hands on her back
His eyes viewing hers
Persuasive words in her ears
Words she wants him to repeat.

An Alert Observer

When she ventures forth
She reads thoughts in others' eyes
Scans, observes, collects,
Pauses, weighs, and considers,
How to gain an advantage.

An Elegant Sham

Though married for years
Only the façade remains
A well-closed curtain
Unfaithfulness stays hidden
Tears shed in secret as well.

An Old Mistress

No longer sleeping
Weary eyes disheveled hair
Pain allows no rest
Yet she would gladly resume
Luring eager wealthy men.

Another Quick Conquest

Handsome, bold, charming,
Not a penny to his name
He flatters her well
She would try to refuse him
But his wit wins her over.

Any Way One Looks at It

He does not venture out
Amusements attract him not
Reality is:
Safely kept in a locked box
His ex-wife has his money.

As if Hovering

Although far away
His wife's words pervade his thoughts
Charming, inviting,
Coaxing, witty, persuasive,
Reproach him for his absence.

As if the Stars Had Aligned

She remembered him
Each pleasing word said to her
How he took her hand
Effortlessly convinced her
During his brief time with her.

As of Now Two People Know

She learned his secrets
Revealed what he had concealed
Now wants him to stay
The two have much to discuss
He will hear each word of hers.

At Regular Intervals

Her hands blindfold him
Soothingly caressingly
Cause him to relax
Once again, succumb to her
Hear each velvet word of hers.

At Times Distracted

She was fond of you
Liked to tease you flirt with you
Offer you her hand
Lead you onto the dance floor
Then take a glance at others.

Banquet Conversation

She found you witty
Adored listening to you
Late into the night
But it ended abruptly
When her husband beckoned.

Best Not to Speak

Please remain silent
This scandal will do no harm
Word should not get out
If you try to cause trouble
You can be implicated.

Brief Distraction

Watch her velvet hand
Follow it as it beckons
Teases and tempts you
Shows off its supple movements
Then quickly slips out of sight.

Briefly Happy

You thought she loved you
She does have fond memories
How you took her hand
Persuaded and embraced her
But her heart wanders freely.

Busted

Her stolid husband
Oh, she took him for a fool
He really bored her
Nonetheless, he was clever
When he caught her in the act.

By Simply Passing By

She can beckon him
Watch as his eyes follow hers
Show him a cute grin
Cause him to yearn endlessly
This man whom she fascinates.

Bygones Are Bygones

She may have fooled him
Kept a few scandals hidden
But never worries,
Once her charms beguile him
He at once agrees with her.

Carefree Fun

As the waves roll in
She lounges in the sunshine
Lets the staff serve her
Lives as the world pleases her
Thanks to prompt blackmail payments.

Caribbean Afternoon

Under azure skies
Showing off her new swimsuit
She lets the time pass
Polite, sharply dressed waiters
Will soon hear her next request.

Caught Utterly Off Guard

She seemed so timid
Scarcely able to converse
No one could have guessed
How she would leave so quickly
With all those pearls in her purse?

Champagne Lady

She loves the bubbly
This effervescent pleasure
Sips and grins at you
Cannot look away from you
May even extend her hand.

Circumspect

She gazes at him
Turns away when he looks back
Observes each detail
Never lets him drift from view
Knows to avoid his wife's eyes.

Coaxing Him to Cooperate

Her hands on his back
Her eyes overlook nothing
Her words in his ear
At times, she must remind him
Of things he wants kept secret.

Common Hollywood Scene

She hoped for stardom
Met with studio people
Even slept with some
Obtained many promises
Now hopes they do not forget.

Completely Averse

Content to be seen
She knows her swimsuit fits well
Enjoys flirting but
Very quickly turns her eyes
Away from her ex-husband.

Completely Mistaken

You thought you knew her
Could always lead her about
Wherever you choose
But she has observed you well
Now has a deal to propose.

Completely Obvious

She knows about you,
How she occupies your thoughts
What you wish to say
How you would gain her favor,
And thinks of another man.

Constant Reassurance

Her soft hands touch him
Gently keeping him in place
Calm his restless mind
She will always be with him
None of his thoughts go unwatched.

Constantly Reminded

Though seemingly calm
A relaxed charming lady
Eager to be seen
Each time she noticed his stare
She recalled what he had done.

Defenseless Victim

She found you handsome
Made sure you knew she liked you
Suggested a tryst
But on the way to her place
She made off with your wallet.

Discomfiting Glance

Now you can see her
Since she fixed her eyes on yours
Catch a glimpse of her
Try to guess her intentions
How much she knows about you.

Discreet Flirting

Her thoughts well hidden
She observes those around her
Takes in all details,
She loves to employ her wit
Someone can be persuaded.

Discreetly Divulged

Although oddly dressed
Known for his pantomime pranks
Once he starts to speak
Confides his thoughts to others
A buffoon can be charming.

Done Quickly and in Secret

Velvet mask in place
Ready for any caper
A cute cat burglar
Filches the ruby necklace
Of his lovely new mistress.

Dreaded Repetition

She knows he sees her
A sly lurking observer
Seemingly inert
All means of attack concealed
Now having found a weakness.

Dreams at Noon

She sits near the sea
Trim figure in her swimsuit
Long flowing dark hair
Gaze fixed to the horizon
Oblivious of men's eyes.

Eager to Turn Away

Aware of his ploy
Understanding his deceit
She averts her gaze
Refuses to say a word
No matter how he insists.

Easily Persuaded

She knows him quite well
Sees him react to her grin
Take her offered hand
Listen to her gentle words
As has happened many times.

Easily Repeated

She likes to charm you
See how your eyes follow her
Speak softly to you
Hold you snugly in her arms
Just to swindle you again.

Embarrassingly Unequal

He asks on his knees
The divorce terms are very harsh
He does need money,
Though she loves to live with him
She will not remarry him.

Excellent Hotel Service

Fresh out of the pool
Expensive swimsuit still soaked
Her cocktail arrives
A spotless gloved hand serves it
She knows his wife is watching.

Expectations Unfulfilled

She likes to fool him
Suggest he can have his way
Let his eyes meet hers
Enjoy seeing his response
Grin and turn away again.

Expected and Unexpected

Unafraid of men
Indeed eager to be seen
She puts them at ease
Gazing at them wistfully
And may choose to favor one.

Fashion Image

We see her on screen
Eyes fixed on the camera
Gazing, enticing,
Ready to extend her hand
Not letting us look away.

Finally Secure

In his wife's embrace
Her velvet hands on his heart
He lets down his guard
Listens to each word she says
How only she keeps him safe.

Finally Succeeding

Touch her velvet hand
You had been staring at it
Of course she noticed
Kept its black sheen in your sight
Knowing how you would respond.

Fleeting Moments

With her witty words
She likes to inveigle him
Tantalize, promise,
Glimpse another man and then
Slowly turn her back to him.

Fleeting Pleasure

Watch as she walks by
Glides across the movie screen
-Elegance, poise, charm-
Focuses her eyes on you
Then abruptly turns away.

Fondly Recalled

As soft music plays
He remembers nights with her
His arms around her
Her hands caressing his face
How neither would let go.

Forewarned

She sees him approach
Confident, overbearing,
Knows what he will say
Each word designed to exploit
Dreads the thought of submitting.

Fortunate Encounter

He beholds her hand
Offered once his eyes meet hers
Lets her entice him
Slowly gently discreetly
She coaxes and convinces.

Fortunes Change Quickly

Though grateful to him
For the gifts he had lavished
She grew bored with him,
When a wealthier man came
She began to flatter him.

Friday at 10 P.M.

He works late tonight
Having nowhere else to go
Much needs to be done
And he prefers not to see
His ex-wife out on the town.

Good Carnival Decision

He did not escape
She had let him meander
Chat with the ladies
Then when he least expected
She appeared and greeted him.

Grasping Justice

Swift lithe villainess
Subtly masked in black velvet
Slips in soundlessly
Surreptitiously seizes
Her husband's girlfriend's jewelry.

Happiness Lost and Found

His ex-wife sees him
As he walks along the beach
Lady at his side
His new wife in her swimsuit
Her hand gently holding his.

Hardly a Sound

All alone tonight
Except for her purring cat
Whom she caresses
And who is faithful to her
Now that her lover has gone.

Hardly a Sound Was Made

With supple gloved hands
She deftly caresses him
Soothes, calms, eases, lulls,
Watches his eyes slowly close
Then snatches his wife's diamonds.

Harsh Justice

He cannot escape
The divorce verdict keeps him
In a legal vise
His ex-wife will not relent
And makes her intentions known.

He Will Be Discreet

Her hands on his neck
A loving velvet caress
On his jugular
She tells him he has new plans
All of which he will accept.

Her Eyes Remain Open

Apparently calm
Even content to be seen
In snug fitting silk
In the midst of revelers
She can see where danger lurks.

Her Favorite Oil Painting

Part of a series
Works of true brilliance
She has the best one
And admires it each day
The museum still has some.

Her Second Husband

Unbeknownst to him
She keeps a very close watch
Carefully observes
Leaves no detail unnoticed
Since she will not be deceived.

His Clever Mistress

Though she is charming
Always eager to please him
She does unnerve him
With a deft touch, she shows him
How she can steal his cuff links.

His First Wife Finds Him

Once her eyes meet his
He hesitates, tries to speak,
Reacts awkwardly,
She pleasantly says hello
Looks at his new wife and leaves.

Hotel Restaurant Scene

Once breakfast concludes
The last drops of coffee sipped
She stares in silence
Remembers the night's pleasures
Wonders how he slipped away.

Idle Hours

He went out tonight
She heard his sports car zoom off
Perhaps a nightclub
Places he is often seen
He will not confide in her.

Impeccable

Her pink party dress
Such smooth inviting contours
Causes men to dream
A wistful nostalgic dream
As they stare at the dance floor.

In Familiar Surroundings

Hands in smooth gloves
Face well and cleverly masked
A smart villainess
Strolls into her lover's home
Deftly swipes his wife's rubies.

Intense Observation

She knows he sees her
Each detail, gesture, nuance,
Briefly, she looks back
His eyes do not turn away
Must see that she looks elsewhere.

Invitation Accepted

The lady's deft hands
Gently untie his necktie
Take his hands in hers
Soon he stares into her eyes
Accepts all that she suggests.

Ipanema Traditions Continue

Leisurely she strolls
Freely caressed by the wind
Each part of her touched
Mostly her relaxed spirit
Her view ventures to the sea.

Irrefutable Proof

A clever husband
Outwitted his trusting wife
At least he thought so
Until her alert eyes found
A forgotten lipstick case.

It Was Not So Much Your Doing

She did seek you out
Arrange to be never far
To be seen with you
Made subtle hints to others
And knew when you would respond.

Joy Lost Not Long Ago

In this empty time
Solitude rediscovered
Silent memories
Sweetness receding from view
Cause her to remember him.

Knowing what You Must Lose

She asks for silence
Already knows what you think
How you have yielded
Why you cannot refuse her
And what she will take from you.

Lady on the Beach

Her face and fine hair
Smooth hands, arms, spirit and heart
Caressed by the breeze
She looks westward to the sea
Dreams of her husband's return.

Left to Consider

He had promised much
Flattered and persuaded her
She was reassured
Looked forward to their future
Now she wonders where he is.

Lingering a Moment

Let her hands tempt you
They extend halfway to you
Invite even tease
Insist that your eyes fixate
Will hold you or slip away.

Major Mistake

You should have guessed it
That sly furtive grin of hers
Did give her away
Yet she fooled you completely
Now where is your wife's necklace?

Meeting in Venice

Beside drained glasses
Empty prosecco bottles
Masked lovers recline
Each unknown to the other
And no language in common.

Merely a Spectator

With a wistful gaze
She stares at her ex-husband
Watches him walk past
Then sees his new wife greet him
Invite him into her car.

Midnight Nears

Her eyes fixed on his
Her velvet hands holding his
His thoughts clear to her
She suggests another dance
After which she will turn in.

Modern Day Calypso

Again in her arms
His gorgeous lady's embrace
He succumbs to her
Gratefully declares his love
She enjoys enchanting him.

Moonstruck

His hands on her hips
Touch her smooth sleek black swimsuit
She fixes her gaze
Gives him a wistful smile
Knows that she has lured him back.

More Memories Return

Velvet on his skin
He yielded to her coaxing
Her hands on his back
She caressed whispered enticed
Then surprised him with a kiss.

More than Enough

With her velvet touch
Calmly applied at midnight
During a slow dance
Under the moon's gentle glow
She deftly wins him over.

Morning Pleasure

As breakfast winds down
She savors his love letter
Finds it delightful
To ponder throughout the day,
She will keep leading him on.

Most at Ease with Herself

Her fans adore her
As she stares from the screen
Each would catch her eye
Yet know that if she sees you
She is most indifferent.

Most Observant

Her dark relaxed eyes
Coupled with easy laughter
Delight and enchant
She sets completely at ease
A man she will soon swindle.

Never at a Distance

In his thoughts again
Her long sleek silk dress in sight
Calm sweet whispered words
Both her velvet hands in his
Her eyes lovingly watch him.

Never at Rest

Though alone right now
Her eyes scan the social scene
See who is with whom
Who has gained advantages
Which weaknesses to exploit.

Never to Be Repeated

He once possessed her
She gladly tried to please him
Fulfilled his wishes
At no time would refuse him
Now she will not speak of him.

Never Unnoticed

Gorgeous and witty
This lady loves to enchant
Flatter and entice
Live as her caprice prefers
Knowing others envy her.

Night Time Approaches

As men gaze at her
She turns her eyes to the sea
To the setting sun
Where in the midst of bright rays
Seagulls venture forth in pairs.

No Anxiety at All

She can persuade him
A bit of charm will suffice,
Once she speaks to him
She knows he will soon agree
Even to remarry her.

No Compromise Possible

Gorgeous, elegant
Both her hands pressing on him
Her eyes fathom his
She holds him safe in her heart
His lady knows his secrets.

No Cracks in the Façade

Not one bit bothered
Even at times disdainful
Of what others think
She never shows a weakness
Though her husband cheats on her.

No Danger Perceived

Once his hand takes hers
He leads and inveigles her
Whispers soothing words
Persuades her with promises
Her worries soon disappear.

No Explanation

He seemed to love her
Sensed and dispelled all her doubts
She was taken in
Gladly believed he would stay,
Now she wonders what happened.

No Hesitation nor Remorse

He focused on her
Noticed how she felt flattered
Tempted with smooth words
Soon had her yielding to him
Then shifted his eyes elsewhere.

No More Illusions Are Possible

Although she loved you
Eagerly waited for you
Gave herself to you
Looked forward to life with you
She came to understand you.

No Need to Say a Word

Now that she is gone
You spend your time pondering
One indiscretion
She chose not to overlook
Though she will not speak of it.

No Obstacle Encountered

Her subtle deft touch
Velvet covering your eyes
Lilting words lull you
Soon enough you go along
And you have been well swindled.

No One Got Caught

She loved him for years
Discreetly and out of sight
No suspicions raised
But as all can clearly see
His new lady holds his hand.

No Warning Possible

Oh yes, she awaits
Fully aware of your thoughts
But unseen by you
None of your deeds forgotten
Soon to exploit a weakness.

Not a Thing to Hide

Now that you see her
Know that she has observed you
Overlooked nothing
Is sure how you will react
Once the conversation starts.

Not Bothered in the Least

As cocktails are served
Her elegance is noticed
All eyes gaze at her
Though she may think to see us
She dreamily looks skyward.

Not Completely Safe

Shielded from men's eyes
Yet still cognizant of them
She remains silent
Content to let others speak
To listen for faint warnings.

Not One Bit Discouraged

Once he jilted her
She felt free from any rules
To roam flirt and tempt
Watch as doors opened for her
Much to her rivals' chagrin.

Not Ready to Forgive

After he fooled her
She remained in the background
A keen observer
Who took grim satisfaction
In each setback he suffered.

Not the First Time

She listens to him
How he explains his actions
Where he was last night
All his justifications
And finds she begins to doubt.

Nothing Hidden

Something is amiss
At this romantic dinner
The man is upset
He sees his wife is wearing
Earrings swiped from his mistress.

Nothing to Be Misunderstood

She must forget him
After all his flattery
Flirting and teasing
Smooth words during slow dances
Clearly he will not return.

Nothing Unobserved

Though she seems carefree
Relaxed and in a good mood
She keeps a close watch
Her gaze fixed on her husband
Whom she can catch unaware.

Noticed Much Later

With a velvet hand
Elegantly gracefully
Smoothly soundlessly
Also imperceptibly
She steals her lover's cufflinks.

Obliged to Sit One Out

The music picks up
He has a new dance partner
One whom he holds close
Who has his full attention
As another must look on.

Observed by the Staff

Her cocktail arrives
She will slowly savor it
Watch others pass by
Note each elegant detail
And do the same tomorrow.

Observing while Unobserved

She likes to watch him
His appearance and manner
Subtle clues he gives
She takes it all in but must
Turn her eyes when he looks back.

Obvious Consternation

She always helped him
Fulfilled each of his requests
Even paid his debts
Yet for all she did for him
He has found a new lover.

Obvious Expectations

She lets him see her
In her new sleek black swimsuit
Snug, wet, glistening,
Smooth, tempting, and inviting,
Of course he will follow her.

On the Boulevard

In their new dresses
Smooth silk carefully measured
They stroll and chat
Think of new stores to visit
Penniless people watch them.

Once Refused

After you left her
She stayed discreetly in sight
Knew where you would look
Understands h ow to tempt you
Yet she turns away each time.

One Forgets, Another Doesn't

Since he betrayed her
She cares not to speak of him
Feigns indifference
Yet nothing eludes her sight
She is never far from him.

One Person Has Decided

She finds you witty
Lets the conversation last
Even past midnight
By which time she knows you well
And whether to chat again.

One-Time Encounter

A masked beauty queen
Sneaks into his hotel room
Just the two of them
Puts a blindfold on him and
Makes off with his wife's necklace.

Only a Bit of Nostalgia

With each sip of gin
She ponders old memories
Flirtatious dances
Witty words from handsome men
Promises of love now gone.

Only a Fool Forgets

True, he once fooled her
Flirted, cajoled and misled,
It all amused him
A simple fun episode
But she will soon take revenge.

Only Recently Acquainted

She stays close to him
Both hands near enough to touch
Listens carefully
Keeps his eyes focused on hers
Soon leads him where she chooses.

Only Two People Understand

She fixes her gaze
Notices how his eyes turn
Briefly glance at her
Show more than a little fear
At what she may choose to say.

Opportunity Seized

The lady's deft hands
Sheathed in delicate velvet
Were safely in his
Suggested how she would yield
Then swiped his wife's wedding ring.

Outwitted

No more words to speak
Each stratagem defeated
Outcome determined
She must grudgingly concede
Behold her rival's triumph.

Painful Disclosure

Yes, the scandal broke
All that she had hoped to hide
Was clearly revealed,
She would look away but sees
A very mischievous grin.

Past Events Unforgotten

He can still see her
A shadowy gray specter
Never far from him
Refusing to be dismissed
Always with words of reproach.

Past the Point of No Return

His mistress beckons
Shows the jewelry he gave her
Silently cajoles
Reminds him of his promise
How he cannot refuse her.

Past Thoughts Remain

Now that he has gone
She can be seen by herself
Wandering homeward
Silent, aloof, hesitant,
At times letting out a sigh.

Perhaps Once Again

She would wait for him
Fondly recalls starlit nights
When he took her hand
Looked deeply into her eyes
To coax and win her favor.

Perhaps to Be Expected

Yes, he once loved her
Tried to flatter and coax her
It seemed she would yield
But she was never constant
New fun times always beckoned.

Plain to See

She can show her face
The witty charm the mask hides
Even fix her gaze
Let her sly grin reveal how
She keeps this victim blackmailed.

Plans Can Change

Her eyes turn to him
Slowly he notices her
Wistful expression
Soulful languid countenance
Invitation for a chat.

Poolside Observation

She likes to watch him
Discreetly keep him in sight
Notice each nuance
Plan how to entice him then
Turn away when he looks back.

Poolside Pause

She lets him kiss her
Place his hands on her swimsuit
Smooth and dripping wet
Then her hands push him away
They will meet again later.

Punishment Given in Venice

No mask could hide her
His wife showed her no mercy
One big push sufficed
Her husband had to hear it:
A loud splash in the canal.

Quickly Overlooked

She tried to please him
Employ all her wit and charm
He did notice her,
Though she offered him her hand
He found her most bothersome.

Ready at All Times

Though at a masked ball
Thoroughly incognito
Her face well concealed
Nobody escapes her view
Certainly not her husband.

Ready for the Next Move

She likes to watch him
Keep her eyes sharply focused
Observe each detail
Think of ways to flirt with him
Since his divorce is pending.

Reckoning

Her eyes fixed on his
Her pleasant voice now silent
Her hands push back his
She has come to understand
All his scandals plain to see.

Remembered Very Well

At times she sees him:
Tattered clothes, unshaven face,
Eyes staring blankly;
He does not know where to turn
This man whose fortune she took.

Reminded Again

You watch her walk past
Still the same elegant look
Shimmering silk dress
Smooth dark hair and alert eyes
Cause you to observe and sigh.

Second Thoughts

He had seemed sincere
With all his well-chosen words
Thoroughly forthright
A man not to be refused,
Only now does she doubt him.

Seemingly Certain Success

She stays in his thoughts
How his hands took hold of hers
Her eyes fixed on his
She seemed glad to yield to him
As if she had planned to stay.

Seen Only Briefly

She would have loved him
Chose her most elegant dress
Placed herself near him
Noticed when his eyes met hers,
But his glance soon turned away.

She Focuses on You

Stare into her eyes
Enjoy this moment she gives,
When she turns away
You will notice every nuance
As she glides across the screen.

She Had Asked Him to Stay

Alone in her house
Soft background music playing
She sits on a couch
Empty champagne glass in hand
Wonders where he is tonight.

She Is Always Mysterious

You try to please her
Yet you must see she remains
Quite indifferent
No secrets will she divulge
Nor try to uncover yours.

She Is Ready to Strike

Eyes sharply focused
Thoughts directed to her aim
All weaknesses found
This lady now steps forward
You will not escape her view.

She Makes the Party Begin

Her life is carefree
Dedicated to pleasure
A whirlwind of fun
She can always have a laugh
Now that she has him blackmailed.

She Must Look Away

Her eyes scanned the scene
Beautiful people poolside
She took it all in
All of it pleased her until
She noticed his wife look back.

She Stays in the Background

Though she could fool him
Playfully lead him astray
Deftly outwit him
Render him fully helpless
She knows to avoid his wife.

She Will Find the Right Moment

She sees you clearly
All your thoughts and intentions
What you have in mind
Knows just how to persuade you
Yet conceals all her secrets.

Sheltered

Though born to great wealth
She chose to remain discreet
Of course, for her son,
She knew to set funds aside
In case her husband left them.

Some Memories Never Fade

Each time you saw her
You were suddenly silent
Almost daydreaming
Perhaps eager to greet her
But she never glanced at you.

Something Will Soon Happen

A cute girl poolside
Scarcely a cent to her name
Yet her ready wit
Words men will eagerly hear
Must disrupt this tranquil scene.

Soon Persuaded

She extends her hand
Focuses her eyes on his
Understands his thoughts
Certain of complete success,
He is quite smitten with her.

Soon to Succeed

She lets men see her
Loves how they view each aspect
At the audition
Oh, how they long to embrace her
And dream of future film scenes.

Sophistication in the Nickelodeon

See her eyes focus
Exclude all else from her view
Let her catch your eye
She stares at you lovingly
Gladly gives you this moment.

Spontaneous Gathering

Past rows of young men
The cute film star makes her way
Her long dark green dress
Matching silk gloves and black hair,
She turns to greet the flash bulbs.

Strength Gained

Yes, she had setbacks
Embarrassing ones even
She forgets nothing
Of course there were lessons learned
No man will fool her again.

Successful Advertising

Slightly out of reach
Yet each bit of wealth displayed
Elegant tasteful
For your obvious pleasure
Of course soon taken from view

Successful Flirting

Her eyes fixed on his
Seeing all he sees and thinks
She has disarmed him
Gives him a sly wistful grin
Lets him gently touch her hand.

Sudden Unpleasant Change

He had promised much
Generously gave her gifts
This new love beckoned
Then money problems arose
And back to his wife he went.

Suddenly Brought to an End

He takes leave of her
Offers his apologies
He did mislead her
She hoped it would go on but
His wife has prerogatives.

Suddenly Dismayed

She truly loved him
Had been generous with him
Forgave all his faults
Determined his future plans
Now sees him with someone else.

Suspicion but Nothing More

Though not in a rush
She tries to keep a brisk pace
Discreet not furtive
Leaving not a thing behind
And hopefully not followed.

Technique Perfected

She knows how to flirt
Make sure your eyes follow her
Gauge your reaction
Suggest that you take her hand
Laugh and turn her back to you.

The Center of Attention

Though many see her
Silk, velvet, pearls, glossy hair,
Her fathoming eyes
Look away from tonight's crowd
Dream of faraway pleasures.

The Hands that Fooled Him

Elegantly sheathed
Shimmering glossy velvet
Dexterous supple
Yet passing fully unseen
As she steals his wife's rubies.

The Lady Has All She Desires

An oceanside home
Well-chosen art in all rooms
Men who call on her
Servants who promptly reply
And her embezzled fortune.

The Lady Sees You Clearly

Though she stares at you
In a quite wistful manner
Try not to look back
She often affects this air
Then lets something distract her.

The Lady Turns Away

It should have worked out
She enjoyed your company
Simply adored you,
A slight indiscretion and
You thought she had not noticed.

The Need to Be Alert

She knows he is there
Not quite overlooking her
Seemingly carefree
As if not thinking of her
Yet eager to try again.

The Trap Has Sprung

Her eyes fixed on him
Her cheerful grin explains all
She knows his secrets
Takes hold of both of his hands
Promises to be discreet.

There Is Justice

He enjoyed the night
In the lovely lady's arms
Far from his wife's eyes
But now he can clearly see
His mistress stole his wallet.

Things Not Yet Foreseen

She listens to him
Understands every word
Observes and ponders
Would like to agree with him
Not knowing where his thoughts lurk.

Though Very Devoted

Oh, yes, she loved him
Gladly let him take her hand
Lead her as he chose
Would have stayed in his embrace
But only as his equal.

Times Have Certainly Changed

It is quite stressful
Enough to make someone faint
She sees his ex-wife
Witty, charming, re-married,
Wearing pearls he once gave her.

Tokens of His Esteem

Silk scarves and dresses
Handbags gloves shoes necklaces
Promises of love
She would have stayed with him but
His wife's lawyer intervened.

Thoughts Unspoken

Though you stepped aside
She knew you were watching her
What you liked to see
How she could coax a smile
Wistful dreams for years to come.

Too Much Information Discovered

She observed him well
Carefully listened to him
He has no secrets
As she discreetly tells him
He must accept her request.

Tossed Aside

She tried to please him
Submitted to his demands
Let him have his way
Offered more but for all that
He dumped her for another.

Traffic Stops

Slowly passing by
Smooth long silk black dress
Shimmering dark hair
Velvet gloves holding her purse
Men may admire her now.

Truly Baffling

Suddenly alone
She still tries to look relaxed
Confident even
Of course, she is attractive
But he left so abruptly.

Trump Card Played

She knows you quite well
Observed and understands you
All you have in mind
What you are eager to do
That is how she swindled you.

Unavoidable Scrutiny

Her eyes follow you
No detail will elude her
Each of your actions
Whatever thoughts cross your mind
Weaknesses you would conceal.

Undeniable Reality

There was no mistake
She saw his other lover
Arm in arm with him
Kissing laughing whispering
Then turning an eye to her.

Understanding an Error

After trusting him
Guessing he would be grateful,
She learned how he is:
Only concerned with himself
Even disdainful of her.

Undetected Danger

Most mysterious
She lurks among revelers
A masked courtesan
Her supple hands in soft gloves
She makes off with emeralds.

Unwisely Succumbing

Once he had lured her
Led her to dance on a string
Captivated her
Caused her to indulge his whims
He kept on demanding more.

Up in Smoke

She was fond of him
Thought that she would marry him
He left abruptly
Seemed to forget her quickly
A new lady came his way.

Utterly Discontented

No lack of money
They own some costly baubles
Their wealth opens doors
Yet their lives are unfulfilled
They will soon bicker again.

Verdict Handed Down

Cannot elude or alleviate
Ruthless divorce decree
Unyielding tightening legal vise
Stonehearted ex-wife relents not
Has insisted on harshness.

Viewed on a Sunny Afternoon

At ease with herself
Aware how others see her
She enjoys her swim,
When she steps out of the pool
She knows eyes will turn to her.

Vital Tools

Those smooth velvet gloves
They make her look elegant
Sophisticated
Ever the witty lady
Even when stealing gemstones.

Vulnerability

Once her hand takes his
In a slow velvet embrace
He must turn to her
She fixes her eyes on him
Reminds him of what she knows.

Waiting in Vain

Her phone has not rung
The long night hours slowly pass
His words come to mind
All the promises he made
How he would soon leave his wife.

What One Can Refuse to Admit

He may have left her
She still ponders, imagines,
Would like to make plans
A day for the two of them
Since she cannot forget him.

What She Retains

Her bracelets and rings
Shown off by her silk black dress
Silver matched with pearls
Have but little value now
Since he found a new mistress.

Who Is Clever?

She may seem naive
Perhaps her husband agrees
But it is not so
The lady keeps a treasure:
His mistress's wedding ring.

Who Is Passing By?

Departing in haste
Discreetly shielding her eyes
She remains silent
Careful to avoid questions
As to whom she left behind.

Why Do You Hesitate?

Let her hands guide you
Take you where it pleases her
She sets you at ease
Lovingly covers your eyes
Speaks of pleasures she offers.

Years after the Divorce

From a safe distance
Careful since he may look back
She fixes her gaze
Lets no detail escape her
Of his new wife at his side.

You Always Succumb

Watch her beckon you
Hear how she will delight you
After luring you,
This time she seems so earnest
Yet she turns away again.

Louis Ed. Fournier.

Mark Schardine is a New Jersey resident with a lifelong love of poetry, and the many pleasures it offers us. He believes that each of us is an heir to the remarkably beautiful tradition of poetry that previous generations have bequeathed to us, and seeks inspiration in works of the past. We must not merely imitate earlier works, but instead experiment with different forms of poetry to explore how old traditions and new experiences can lead to creativity.

In 2015, he published a French language book of his poems, entitled *Au bord des rêves*, and in 2019, it was followed by *Vers des horizons lointains*. He has written three English language books, *Charm, Elegance, and Intrigue*, first published in 2019 and with this new edition in 2023, *As if in a Distant Dream*, published in 2020, and *Under Watchful Eyes* in 2022.

.